Charisma Cat had a wicked idea,
"take the fawns from all the deer."
"I will have complete control,
Of how the cubs and puppies grow."
"Little ones of either gender,
At the Saving Puppy Center."

"Cows, cats, dogs, whole flocks,
We will let coyotes adopt."
"We can't leave these babies alone."
"Babies deserve a loving home."
"Coyotes love a tasty meal,
Turn baby calves into veal."

Stand Up Bear had a big personality,
So he tried his luck with late night comedy.
Telling jokes was his craft,

He made lions and hyenas laugh.
Animals would watch with glee,
To hear the truths that he would speak.

"Bunnies, puppies, and things that moo,
Coyotes turn them into stew."
"How could animals be such dupes,
Coyotes just want piglet soups."
Stand Up Bear got many laughs,
For his defense of a little calf.

The next day the local Roosters,
Reported "Stand Up Bear's a loser."
"We must silence this loud-mouth yuppie,
"He is against saving puppies."
"All who challenge the Saving Puppy Center,
Must have their thought crimes censored."
"Tell the Bear he must leave,"
He can't do stand-up comedy."

Stand Up Bear was not deterred,
He called the local mountain bluebirds
"Carry my message as far as you reach
Carry my message with tweets, tweets tweets."
The blue birds flew all over the farm,
Tweet by tweet to sound the alarm.
"Don't trust the Roosters, they think they are slick, Roosters are animals of deception & tricks."

The Roosters reported,
"the Bears anti-bird."
"We can't let him speak
such dangerous words."
"He talks about turning
calves into veal,
How does that make
farm animals feel?"
"The time has come to
limit his reach,
No longer can he send
such insensitive
tweets."

Stand Up Bear refused to back down,
He would spread his message all over town.
He wrote his jokes for all that would look,
He put his face on the front of a book.
"Who lies around all day and is really fat,
None other than Charisma Cat."

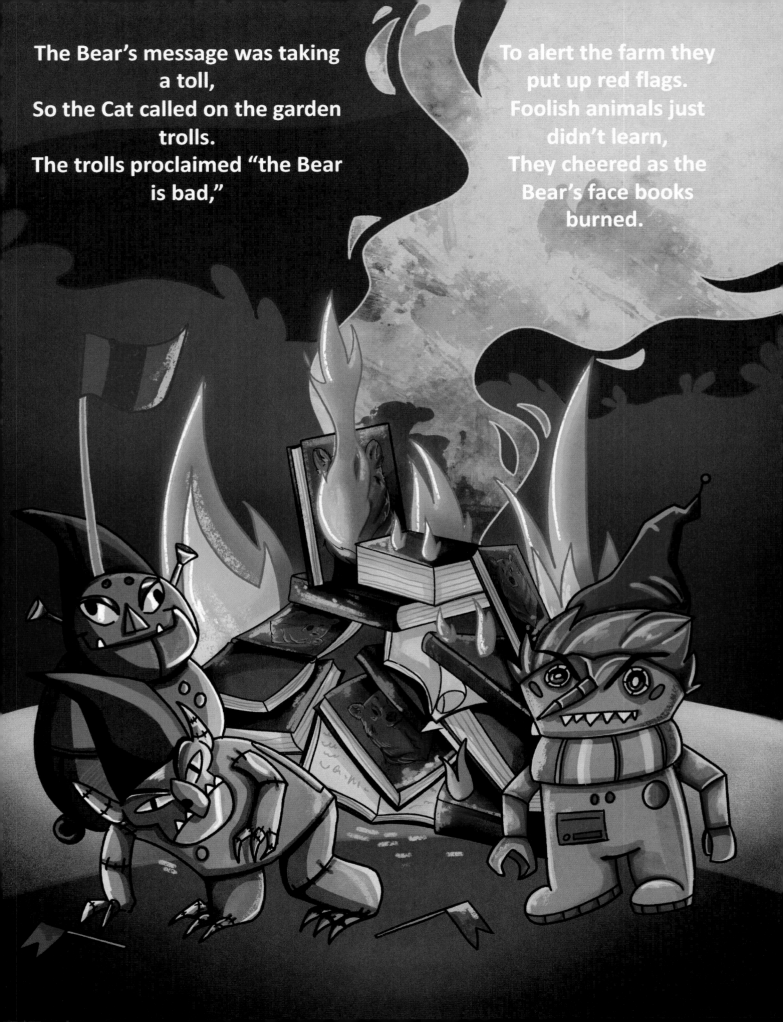

Stand Up Bear had another move,
He took his jokes to the Me and
You Tube.

"Hey guys, did you hear
that rat?
Oh wait, that is Charisma
Cat."
"Who lives with their mom
but wants to sacrifice foals,
Just your average garden
trolls."

Many animals ignored what was true,
And instead decided to signal virtue.
The Bears didn't listen, as other animals did,
The goats would sacrifice all of their kids.
Cows, alpaca, and roly-polies,
Handed their children to hungry coyotes.

Stand Up Bear continued to crush,
And told his jokes at breakfast and lunch.
Nothing can stop him from speaking the truth,
And his message is now reaching the youth.
Speak truth that others would not dare,
And you too will be a stand-up Bear.

Made in United States
Orlando, FL
01 October 2024